REDUCE,
REUSE,
RECYCLE!

Water

Jen Green

WAYLAND

First published in 2009 by Wayland

Copyright © Wayland 2009

Wayland
338 Euston Road
London NW1 3BH

Wayland Australia
Level 17/207 Kent Street
Sydney NSW 2000

Editor: Katie Powell
Designer: Elaine Wilkinson
Illustrator: Ian Thompson
Consultant: Kate Ruttle
Picture Researcher: Shelley Noronha
Photographer: Andy Crawford

British Library Cataloguing in Publication Data
 Green, Jen
  Water. - (Reduce, reuse, recycle!)
  1. Water reuse - Juvenile literature 2. Waste minimization
  - Juvenile literature
  I. Title
  363.7'284

ISBN: 978 0 7502 5712 1

Cover: UpperCut Images/Getty Images

1 Image Source/Getty Images, 2 Wayland Picture Library, 4 NASA, 5 Ecoscene / photog, 7 Stone+ / Getty Images, 8 Image Source/Getty Images, 9 Jim Nicholson / Alamy, 10 ImageShop/Corbis Corporation/ImagePick, 11 © Steven Gillis/LOOP IMAGES/Getty images, 12 Wayland Picture Library, 13 Peter Cade/Getty Images, 14 ISTOCK, 15 Wayland Picture Library, 16 Stockbyte/Photolibrary.com, 17 ISTOCK, 18 © Jennie Woodcock/Reflections/Corbis, 19 Wayland Picture Library, 20 © Jennie Woodcock/Reflections/Getty Images, 21 UpperCut Images/Getty Images, 22 © Fabio Cardoso/Corbis, 23 Kraig Scarbinsky/Getty Images, 24 Stockbyte/Photolibrary.com, 25 © Heide Benser/zefa/Corbis, 26 © MM Productions/Corbis, 27 Recycle Now, 28 t Stockbyte/photolibrary.com, 28 b, 29 t, c, b Wayland Picture Library With thanks to RecycleNow.

The author and publisher would like to thank the following models: Lawrence Do of Scotts Park Primary School, Sam Mears and Madhvi Paul.

Printed in China

Wayland is a division of Hachette Children's Books, an Hachette UK company.
www.hachette.co.uk

Contents

Words in **bold** can be found in the glossary.

Watery planet

Fresh water is important for life. Most of the Earth's surface is covered with water, but nearly all of that is salty seawater, which would make you ill if you tried to drink it. Less than three per cent of Earth's water is fresh, and most of that is ice.

▲ Earth looks blue from space because it is mostly covered by seas and oceans.

Water has three forms: liquid water, invisible **moisture** in the air called **water vapour**, and ice, which is **frozen** water.

Did You Know?

Plants, animals and people all need water, but people often waste it. We can help save water by following the 3 R's – **reduce**, **reuse** and **recycle**. Reducing means using less of something. Reusing is when something is used again, for example when kitchen water is reused in the garden. Recycling is when water is cleaned so it can be used again.

◀ All animals, such as these zebra, need water to survive.

Circling water

The water on our planet is always moving, circling between the land, sea and air. This is called the **water cycle**. As the sun warms the sea, water rises into the air as water vapour. This is called **evaporation**. The moisture turns into tiny water **droplets**, which gather to make clouds.

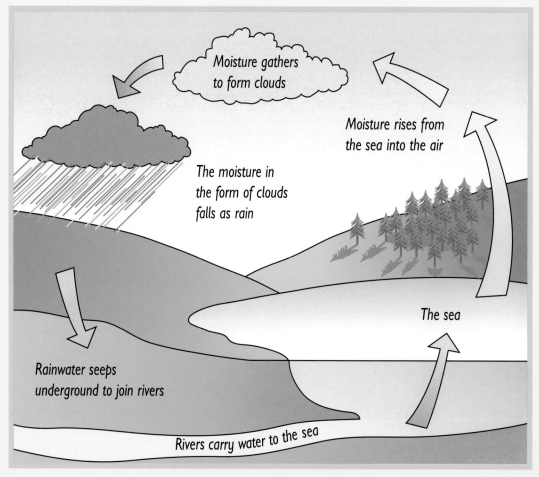

Moisture gathers to form clouds

Moisture rises from the sea into the air

The moisture in the form of clouds falls as rain

The sea

Rainwater seeps underground to join rivers

Rivers carry water to the sea

◀ This diagram shows the water cycle.

When clouds shed
rain, plants and trees
soak up water. The rest trickles
into the ground or into lakes and
rivers. Rivers return water to the
sea to complete the water cycle.
This natural recycling
has gone on
for millions
of years.

▼ *Water evaporates from lakes in the sunshine.*

Water for life

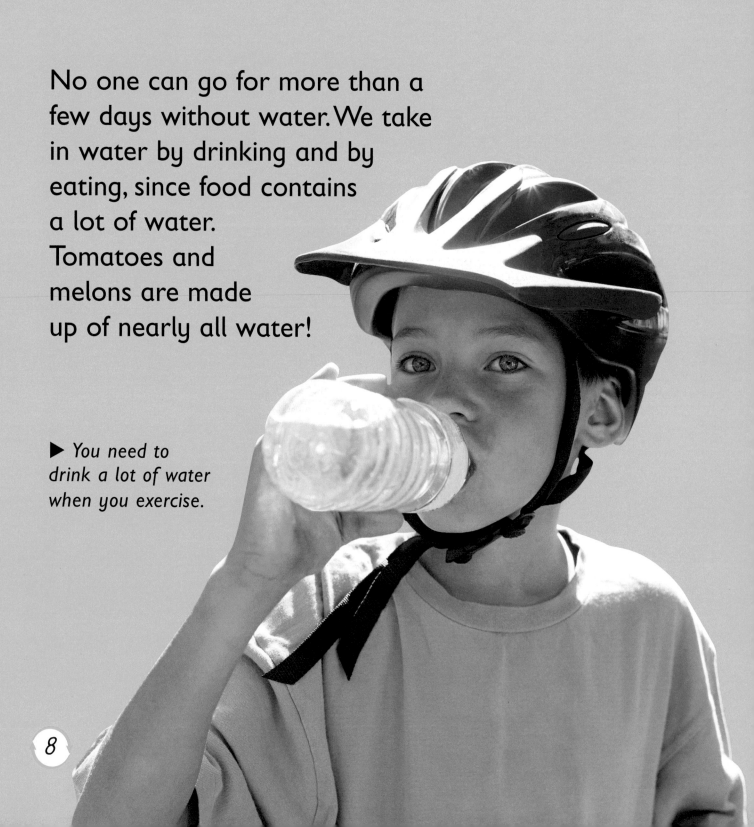

No one can go for more than a few days without water. We take in water by drinking and by eating, since food contains a lot of water. Tomatoes and melons are made up of nearly all water!

▶ *You need to drink a lot of water when you exercise.*

You need to replace the water you lose. We lose water as we exercise, through sweat, as we breathe out and when we go to the toilet.

▼ On a cold day the moisture you breathe out turns back into tiny water droplets that you can see.

Did You Know?

About 65 per cent of your body is made up of water.

Water and work

Water has hundreds of uses. Farmers use huge amounts of it to look after their animals and wet their crops. Water flowing in rivers provides drinking water. People usually dam the river to save water. The lake that forms behind the dam is called a **reservoir**.

◀ A cow has to drink 4 litres of water to produce 1 litre of milk.

Factories use water
for washing, cooling and
making everything from drinks
cans to newspapers. It takes at
least 30 litres of water to make a
newspaper, and 100 litres to make
one drinks can which holds
just a small amount
of fizzy drink!

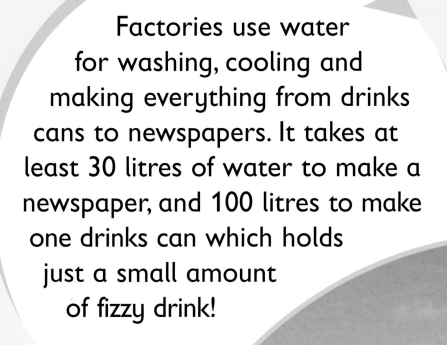

▶ Reservoirs
supply cities
with the water
they need.

Reduce, reuse, recycle

The amount of water in the world has stayed about the same for millions of years, but the number of people on Earth is growing and they need more water. It is important to use water carefully, so there is enough for everyone and everything that needs it.

▶ A dripping tap can waste a litre of water an hour – that adds up to a bathful a week!

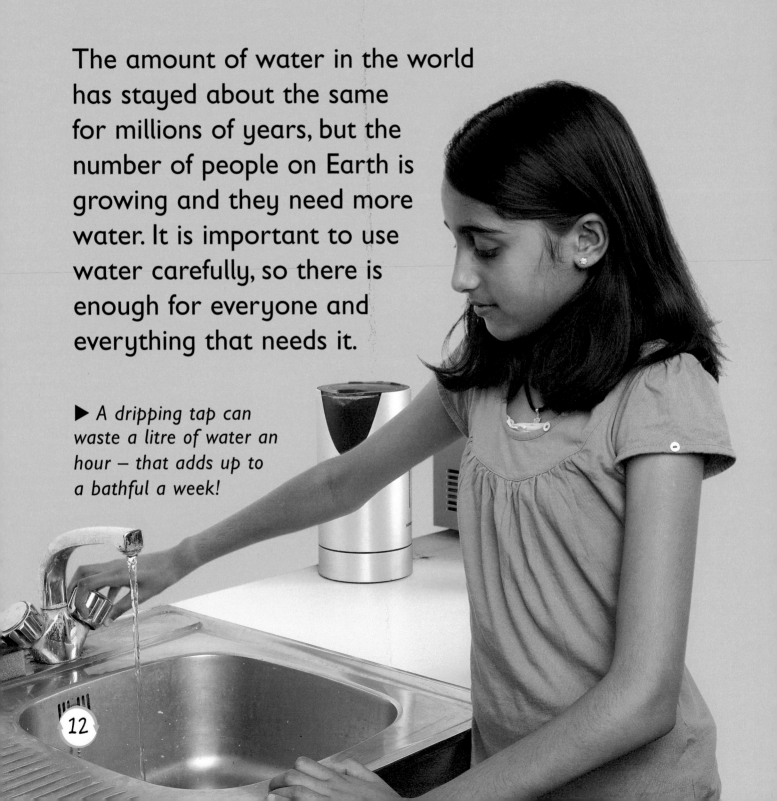

▶ Use a basin of water to wash your hands instead of running the tap.

You Can Help!

Dripping taps waste water. Make sure you turn taps off properly.

There are many ways you can reuse and recycle water. You can also reduce the amount of water you use. For example, don't run the tap while brushing your teeth and don't flush the toilet more than necessary.

Sharing water

Some parts of the world get a lot of rain, so there is plenty of water. Other places get very little rainfall, so people often have to make do using little water. Deserts are places that receive very little rain.

◀ *The Grand Canyon in the United States of America (USA) gets very little rain.*

The wettest town in the USA is Quillayute, Washington, which receives 264 centimetres (104 inches) of rain a year. The driest town is Yuma, Arizona, with just 6.6 centimetres (2.6 inches) a year.

MEASURING RAINFALL

1. Make a rain gauge to measure rainfall by cutting a plastic bottle in half. Ask an adult to help you do this. Put the top half upside-down inside the bottom half to make a funnel.

2. Tape a ruler to the side.

3. Dig a small hole outside for the rain gauge to sit in, so it does not fall over.

▲ Take readings once a week, and empty the rain gauge. Add the weekly totals each month. Make a chart to record rainfall through the year.

Water on tap

The water we use comes from rivers, lakes and reservoirs. In some countries, such as Britain, the water is cleaned and then pumped to our homes. Water flows out of the tap whenever we need it. In other countries people often have to share one tap, or walk a long way to fetch water.

▲ *This young girl has walked for more than an hour to get water and will have to carry it home in heavy containers.*

In Europe, everyone uses about 300 litres of water a day. That is enough to fill two bathtubs! In the USA people use more — about 500 litres. In poor countries, where there is little water, people use less than 50 litres a day.

In rich countries, we use a huge amount of water every day. Cleaning and pumping water is expensive and uses **energy**. In poor countries, people get by with much less water. Wherever you live, it is important to use water carefully.

▼ Using a car wash wastes a lot of water.

How do we use water?

Think about all the ways you use water at home and school. Families and schools use water for washing, drinking, cooking and cleaning. Taking a shower, cleaning your teeth and filling a kettle all use water. The central heating system that keeps you warm also contains water.

▼ *Baths and washing machines use a lot of water.*

18

WATER USE CHART

1. Make a chart to record water use at home over one weekend.

2. List all the ways that your family uses water under headings such as, 'Cleaning teeth', 'Washing-up' and 'Using the toilet'.

3. Ask family members to tick a column each time they use water.

4. Use the chart to work out how much water your family uses in two days.

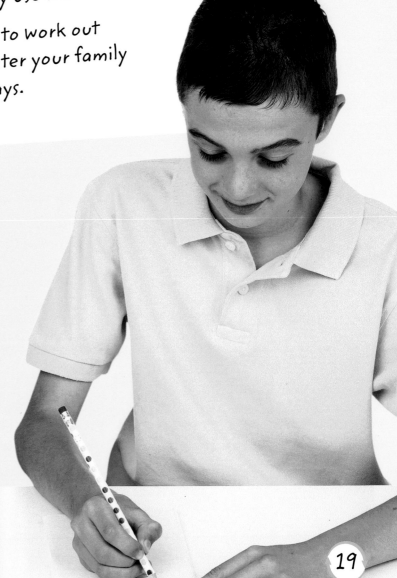

▼ This boy is starting to make his own 'water use chart'.

Did You Know?

• Cleaning your teeth or washing your face and hands uses 5 litres of water

• Flushing the toilet uses 10 litres

• A five-minute shower uses 30 litres

• A full bath uses 120 litres

• Washing-up by hand uses 5-10 litres

• A dishwasher uses 45 litres

Water for washing

A lot of the water we use is for washing. We use water to clean our bodies and our clothes. We also use water to clean bikes and cars outdoors. You can reduce the amount of water you use and still keep clean!

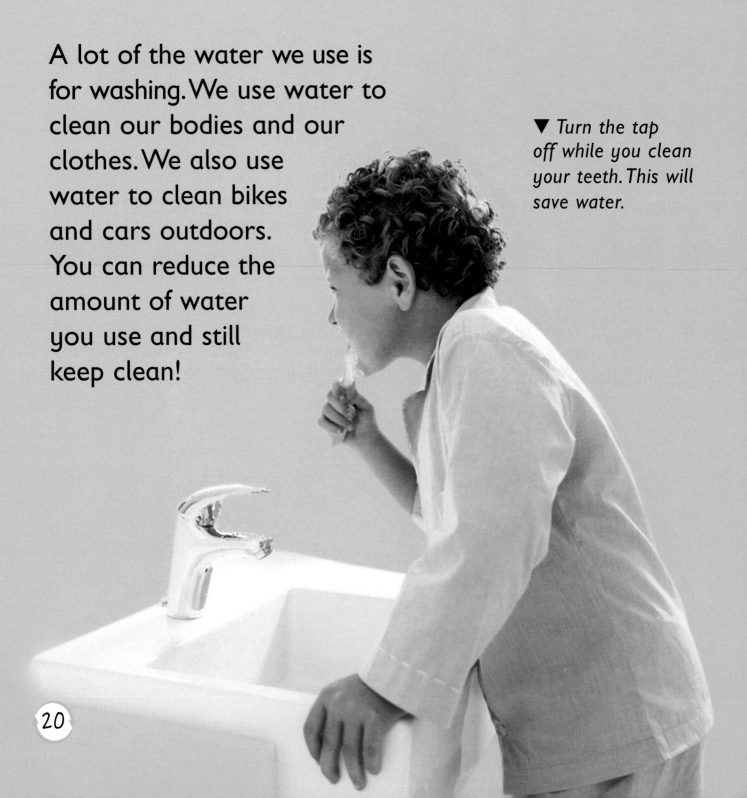

▼ *Turn the tap off while you clean your teeth. This will save water.*

SAVING WASHING WATER

1. Take a quick shower instead of having a bath.

2. Put the plug in before you wash your hands and face, do not use running water.

3. Ask an adult to make sure the washing machine is full before it is used. That way, your family will do fewer washes.

▶ Use a bucket of water to wash the car, instead of a hosepipe or a car wash.

In the kitchen

In the kitchen we use water for all sorts of everyday things. We use water to make drinks, wash and cook food, and clean up afterwards. There are lots of ways to save water in the kitchen. If everyone saved just a little, it would add up to a huge amount.

▼ *Water used for rinsing plates can be reused in the garden.*

▶ *Dishwashers use a lot more water than washing-up by hand.*

SAVING KITCHEN WATER

1. Rinse dirty plates and glasses in a bowl of water, not under a running tap.

2. Wash fruit and vegetables in a bowl of water, too.

3. Ask an adult to wait until the dishwasher is full before using it. Then you will do fewer washes.

Down the drain

The water that goes down the drain contains **sewage**, and also soap, **bleach** and other cleaning products. It has to be cleaned before it flows back into streams and rivers, but cleaning water is expensive. We should try to reduce the amount of dirty water that flows down the drain in the first place.

▲ *Sewage contains harmful **germs** that can cause **disease** and make people and animals ill.*

REDUCING WATER

1. Ask an adult to place a plastic bottle full of water in the **cistern** tank of your toilet. The bottle takes up space in the cistern so less water is used with every flush.

2. Do not use more soap than you need when washing your hands.

3. Do not play in water sprinklers as it wastes water.

▶ Playing in water sprinklers is a lot of fun, but it wastes a lot of water.

In the garden

We use lots of water in the garden, particularly if we water plants with a sprinkler. A sprinkler can use as much water in an hour as a whole family uses in a day! Using a watering can instead reduces the amount of water used outdoors.

◄ Plants in flower beds need less water than plants in pots and hanging baskets.

▼ *Buy a **water butt** to save rainwater. Fill your watering can from the butt.*

You Can Help!

If you water the garden in hot, sunny weather, most of the moisture disappears before plants have a chance to soak it up. Water in the evening instead.

SAVING WATER IN THE GARDEN

1. Save water from washing fruit and vegetables, and rinsing dishes to water the garden.

2. Ask your parents to think about buying plants that do not mind dry **conditions** such as rock roses, heather and lavender.

3. Put **compost** on flower beds to reduce evaporation. That way plants will need less water.

27

Make a water filter

At a **water treatment plant**, water is cleaned by being filtered through sand and gravel. Make your own water filter to see how this works.

YOU WILL NEED:

- two jars,
- a funnel,
- coffee filter papers,
- a little clean sand,
- some gravel,
- some soil.

1. Put a filter paper in the funnel and stand the funnel in a jar.

2. Mix a little soil with water in another jar. Empty the dirty water into the funnel. Look to see how clean the water is.

3. Put a new filter in the funnel. Add a handful of sand and gravel. Pour more dirty water into the funnel. Repeat step 2.

4. The water should be cleaner this time.

WARNING
The filtered water may look clean, but it's not really clean, so don't drink it.

Further information

Topic map

HISTORY

The ancient Egyptians were among the first people to channel water into fields. Find out more about the ancient Egyptians by using a library or the Internet.

GEOGRAPHY

The water that gushes from the tap comes from local rivers, lakes and reservoirs. Look at a local map to find out where there are rivers, lakes and reservoirs in your local area.

MATHS

Look back at your water use chart (page 19). Divide the total for two days by two and multiply by 365 to find out how much water you use in a year.

ENGLISH

Write a story or poem about the water cycle, perhaps from the point of view of a water droplet.

ART/DESIGN

Design a poster explaining why we should all use water carefully and try to reduce, reuse and recycle!

RELIGIOUS STUDIES

Water is used in religious ceremonies by Christians, Muslims, Hindus and other faiths. Can you find out how and why water is used in these religions?

Further reading

Environment Action: Save Water by Kay Barnham (Wayland, 2008)
Good for Me: Water by Sally Hewitt (Wayland, 2007)
Improving Our Environment: Saving Water by Jen Green (Wayland, 2005)
Our Earth: The Water Cycle by Jen Green (Wayland, 2007)

Websites

www.wateraid.org/uk/
A charity that helps people in poor countries get access to water.

www.epa.gov/ebtpages/water.html
Information for children on recycling and reducing water usage in the USA.

www.savewater.com.au/
Lots of tips on how to save water.

www.worldwatercouncil.org/
This website looks at all the different issues surrounding water.

www.sas.org.uk/
Campaign for clean water.

Glossary

bleach	a powerful cleaning product	**sewage**	dirty water from homes, containing chemicals and human waste
cistern	the small tank above the toilet which holds water for flushing	**water butt**	a large container used to store water outdoors
compost	natural materials which rot to make fertiliser for the garden	**water cycle**	the constant movement of water around Earth
condition	the state something is in	**water treatment plant**	a place where water is cleaned so it is safe to drink
disease	an illness		
droplet	a tiny drop		
energy	the power to do work	**water vapour**	moisture in the form of a gas
evaporation	when water changes from a liquid into a gas		
fresh water	water that is not salty		
frozen	when water is cold it turns to ice		
germ	a tiny living thing that can make you ill		
moisture	wetness		
recycle	when water is cleaned for reuse		
reduce	to make something smaller or use less of it		
reservoir	a man-made lake used to store water		
reuse	when something is used again		

Index

Numbers in **bold** refer to a photograph.